AMERICAN LEGENDS™

Sally Hemings

Frances E. Ruffin

The Rosen Publishing Group's
PowerKids Press™
New York

In memory of my mother

Published in 2002 by The Rosen Publishing Group, Inc.
29 East 21st Street, New York, NY 10010

First Edition

Book Design: Michael de Guzman

Project Editor: Kathy Campbell

Photo Credits: p. 4 © North Wind Pictures; p. 7 © Owen Franken/CORBIS; p. 8 © Michael Maslan Historic Photographs/CORBIS; p. 11 © North Wind Pictures; p. 12 © North Wind Pictures; p. 15 © Bettmann/CORBIS; p. 15 © Archivo Iconografico, S.A./CORBIS; p. 16 © Bettmann/CORBIS; p. 19 © Nathaniel K. Gibbs/Monticello; p. 20 © Buddy Mays/CORBIS.

Ruffin, Frances E.
Sally Hemings / Frances E. Ruffin —1st ed.
    p. cm. — (American legends)
Includes bibliographical references (p.   ) and index.
ISBN 0-8239-5828-0 (library binding)
1. Hemings, Sally—Juvenile literature. 2. Women slaves—United States—Biography—Juvenile literature.
3. Slaves—United States—Biography—Juvenile literature. 4. Jefferson, Thomas,1743–1826—Relations with women—Juvenile literature. 5. Jefferson, Thomas, 1743–1826—Relations with slaves—Juvenile literature. [1. Hemings, Sally. 2. Slaves.
3. African Americans—Biography. 4. Women—Biography. 5. Jefferson, Thomas, 1743–1826.]
I. Title. II. American legends (New York, N.Y.)
E332.2 .R84 2002
973.4'6'092—dc21

                                                                                    2001000610

Manufactured in the United States of America

Contents

Thomas Jefferson wrote the Declaration of Independence. Although Jefferson owned slaves, including Sally Hemings, he seemed to be against slavery. He wrote, "Nothing is more certainly written in the book of fate than that these people are to be free."

Sally Hemings

The story of Sally Hemings is also part of the story of the third president of the United States, Thomas Jefferson. Sally Hemings was a **slave** who lived and worked for 52 years at Monticello. Monticello was the Virginia home and **plantation** of Thomas Jefferson. From 1790 to 1808, Sally gave birth to seven children. Jefferson is believed to have been the father of Sally's children. Thomas Jefferson once wrote that slavery is "an **abominable** crime." He also believed that by keeping his slaves, he protected them from harm. Some people, however, claim that his views are **hypocritical**. Jefferson wrote in the Declaration of Independence that "all men are created equal."

What Is a Legend?

Starting in 1802, there were **rumors** that Sally Hemings and President Thomas Jefferson had a special **relationship**. These rumors are part of written and **oral** histories that have become **legends** about their lives. A legend is a story that has been handed down from the past. Some of the information that we have about Sally Hemings is based on Jefferson's own records. Other information is based on letters that mention her, such as those written by Abigail Adams, wife of John Adams, the second president of the United States. Much about Sally's life, though, comes to us through the memories of her children and the people who lived and worked with her, as retold by them.

Reading or hearing about legends is fun. Legends can be based on real people or events. Some can be entirely made up. Most of the stories about Sally's life are true and came from stories retold by her children and the people who knew her.

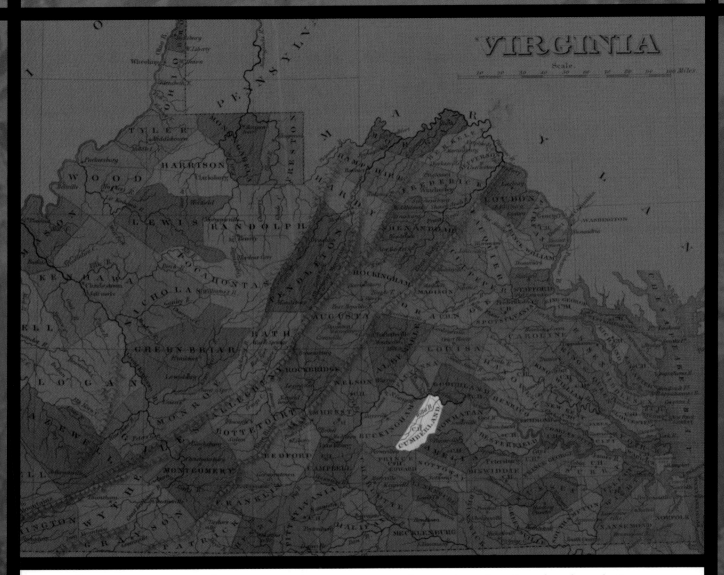

Sally Hemings was born into slavery on a plantation in Cumberland County, Virginia. Sally's father was the plantation owner, John Wayles. Her mother was the slave named Elizabeth Hemings.

A Beginning in Virginia

Sally Hemings was born on a plantation in Cumberland County, Virginia, in 1773. Although she was known always as Sally, her real name might have been Sarah. Sally's grandfather was Captain John Hemings, a captain of an English ship. Her grandmother was an African woman who had been sold as a slave to John Wayles, a Virginia plantation owner. Captain Hemings loved Sally's grandmother. Before Sally's mother was born in 1735, Captain Hemings wanted to buy Sally's grandmother from John Wayles. He wanted to take her and her baby back to England, but John Wayles kept the woman and baby. He believed that they would be valuable as slaves.

An Inheritance

Sally Hemings's mother, Elizabeth, grew up as a slave on John Wayles's plantation. Although he was a married man, Wayles became the father of Elizabeth's children, including her youngest daughter, Sally.

A daughter of John Wayles and his wife married Thomas Jefferson in 1772. Martha Wayles Jefferson was Sally Hemings's half sister. Wayles died in 1773, and left a very large **inheritance** to Martha and Thomas Jefferson. This inheritance was 11,000 acres (4,452 ha) of land and 135 slaves, including Elizabeth Hemings and her children.

This picture shows the Jefferson family's slaves in 1789, welcoming Thomas Jefferson, his daughter, and Sally Hemings back from their stay in Paris.

Sally was about two years old when she and her family moved to Thomas Jefferson's home at Monticello. Sally's mother, Elizabeth, became Mrs. Jefferson's housekeeper. As a young child, Sally helped around the house, too.

Life at Monticello

Sally Hemings was about two years old when her family was moved to Monticello near Charlottesville, Virginia. She and her mother and older sisters and brothers lived in several log cabins on a road called Mulberry Row. Sally's mother was the **housekeeper** at Monticello. Some of Sally's brothers were cooks, gardeners, carpenters, and furniture makers. Some of her sisters were weavers who made cloth and seamstresses who made clothes. Others were "lady's maids" who worked in the home and helped Mrs. Martha Jefferson and her children. As a small girl, Sally ran errands for Mrs. Jefferson.

Voyage to Paris

Martha Jefferson died in 1782. She left behind her 39-year-old husband, Thomas, and her daughters, Martha, Maria, and Lucy. Sally Hemings had become Maria's **companion**. When Jefferson became the American **minister** to France in 1784, he took his oldest daughter, Martha, and some servants. He later sent for Maria. Sally was responsible for taking Maria to her father in Europe. Sally and Maria were both 14 years old. In 1787, the girls stopped first in England and stayed with John Adams, the American minister to England, and his wife, Abigail. Mrs. Adams was surprised that young Sally had such a responsibility. "[Sally] seems fond of the child and appears good natured," Mrs. Adams wrote.

Top: *Abigail Adams lived in England in 1787. When Sally Hemings and Maria Jefferson made their trip to Europe in 1787, they visited Abigail and her husband, John.* Bottom: *Sally visited sites such as this park at the Palace of Versailles in Paris, France.*

King Louis XVI and Queen Marie Antoinette, of France, are seen here with their family. The country of France did not allow slavery. Sally could have remained in France to become a free person, but she did not want to leave her family forever.

A Chance to Be Free

France was a new world for Sally. It did not allow slavery. Thomas Jefferson paid Sally a small wage of $2 each month while she was there. Sally's brother James was the head cook at the mansion that served as Jefferson's home. James was paid $4 every month. James told Sally that by not returning to America, they would be free people. She considered staying but knew she would miss her mother and sisters. Jefferson promised Sally that if she returned to America, she would live a life of **privilege**. Any children she might have would be freed when they became 21. It is believed that Sally and Thomas began a relationship in Paris. In 1789, Jefferson, his daughters, and Sally returned to America, but her brother stayed behind.

Sally and Thomas's Children

Thomas Jefferson had a special room built for Sally in his home at Monticello. Sally also kept a home on Mulberry Row at Monticello, where many of the slave families lived in log cabins. Sally was responsible for caring for Jefferson's clothes and room. In 1790, Sally gave birth to a son, Thomas. People remarked that the baby had very fair skin and red hair, much like Thomas Jefferson's. When young Thomas was a teenager, he was sent to live with relatives of Jefferson's who were named Woodson. Sally had several other children, including two daughters and a son who died in early childhood, a son, Beverly, born in 1798, a daughter, Harriet, born in 1801, and sons Madison and Eston, born in 1805 and 1808.

This is a picture of Mulberry Row at Monticello. Sally had a home here, even though Jefferson had a special room built for her in his mansion.

Thomas Jefferson's grave is located in the Jefferson family cemetery at Monticello. Sally Hemings's descendants believe they should be allowed to be buried there, too.

A Debate

Sally Hemings remained a slave at Monticello until Thomas Jefferson's death in 1826. A year later, Sally moved to Charlottesville, Virginia. She lived with her sons Madison and Eston until her death in 1835. She had never married. No one has ever been able to locate her grave. Sally's many **descendants** have always believed that they were Thomas Jefferson's children. Others, including descendants of Jefferson's daughter Martha Jefferson Randolph, rejected that belief. A **debate** grew between the two groups. The Hemings family believed that they should be recognized as Jefferson's descendants. They also believed that they should have a right to be buried in the Jefferson family cemetery at Monticello.

A Family Reunion

In 1998, **genetic** tests on blood donated by the descendants of Sally Hemings and Martha Jefferson Randolph proved that Thomas Jefferson was the father of at least one of Sally's children and quite possibly all of them. Some people did not accept the scientific proof. Others were relieved to know that their oral history was true. This was welcome news for people, black and white, on both the Sally and Martha sides of Jefferson's family. It also made news worldwide. On May 15, 1999, history was made when more than 80 members of both sides of Thomas Jefferson's and Sally Hemings's families met for a family reunion at Monticello. It was a new beginning for this family.

Glossary

abominable (uh-BAH-mih-nuh-bul) Something that is sickening or hateful.

companion (kum-PAN-yun) A person who shares another person's life.

debate (dih-BAYT) To argue or discuss.

descendants (dih-SEN-dents) People born of a certain family or group.

genetic (jih-NEH-tik) Relating to the science that deals with the passing of traits from a parent or parents to their children.

housekeeper (HOWS-kee-pur) Someone who cares for a house.

hypocritical (hih-puh-KRIH-tih-kuhl) The act of pretending to be one sort of person but behaving differently.

inheritance (in-HEHR-uh-tens) Property or money, received usually from a person who has died.

legends (LEH-jends) Stories passed down through the years that many people believe, but that might not be entirely true.

minister (MIH-nuh-stir) A person who represents their country in a foreign land.

oral (OR-el) Not written; using speech.

plantation (plan-TAY-shun) A very large farm. Many plantation owners used slaves to work their farms.

privilege (PRIHV-lij) A special right or favor.

relationship (rih-LAY-shun-ship) A connection between two or more people.

rumors (ROO-murz) Stories that are heard by a lot of people and that have no proof that they are true.

slave (SLAYV) A person who is "owned" by another person and is forced to work for him or her.

Index

Web Sites

To learn more about Sally Hemings, check out these Web sites:
www.jefferson-hemings.org/
www.monticello.org/plantation/Sally_Hemings.html